S. S. CYRIL & METHODIUS SCHOOL

HARTFORD, CONN.

BRETT HULL

BRETT HULL

Hockey's Top Gun

Margaret J. Goldstein

Lerner Publications Company ■ Minneapolis

To Tom Raber, one heck of a cool guy

This edition of this book is available in two bindings:
Library binding by Lerner Publications Company
Soft cover by First Avenue Editions
241 First Avenue North
Minneapolis, Minnesota 55401

LIBRARY OF CONGRESS CATALOGING-IN-PUBLICATION DATA

Goldstein, Margaret J.
  Brett Hull : hockey's top gun / Margaret J. Goldstein.
      p.   cm.
  Summary: A biography of St. Louis Blues hockey star
Brett Hull.
  ISBN 0-8225-0544-4 (lib. bdg.)
  ISBN 0-8225-9599-0 (pbk.)
  1. Hull, Brett, 1964-   —Juvenile literature. 2. Hockey
players—Canada—Biography—Juvenile literature. 3. St.
Louis Blues (Hockey team)—Juvenile literature. [1. Hull,
Brett, 1964-   . 2. Hockey players.] I. Title.
GV848.5.H82G65   1992
796.962'092—dc20
[B]   91-14822
                                                              CIP
                                                               AC

Copyright © 1992 Lerner Publications Company
Third printing 1995 contains updated information

All rights reserved. International copyright secured. No part of this book may be
reproduced or transmitted in any form or by any means, electronic or mechanical,
including photocopying and recording, or by any information storage or retrieval
system, without permission in writing from the publisher, except for the inclusion of
brief quotations in an acknowledged review.

Manufactured in the United States of America

3   4   5   6   7   8   9   10   –   P/MA   –   01   00   99   98   97   96   95

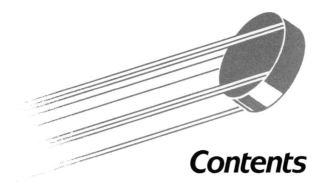

Contents

Brett tries to slip past the Red Wing defense.

50/50 Vision

St. Louis Blues right wing Brett Hull was frustrated as he circled the hockey rink at the Joe Louis Arena in Detroit, Michigan. The Detroit Red Wing defensemen had hassled Brett all night. The second period was almost over, and Number 16 Hull had been able to take only two shots on the Detroit goal.

The Blues had a 6-2 lead over their opponents. The game was well in hand. But on this night, January 25, 1991, Brett was concerned with more than just the outcome of the hockey game.

If Brett could score 50 goals in the first 50 games of the National Hockey League season, he would join an elite group of hockey players. Only Wayne Gretzky, Maurice Richard, Mario Lemieux, and Mike Bossy had ever reached the 50-50 mark.

This was the 49th game of the 1990-91 season, and Brett had scored 48 goals. The pressure was on.

Despite the pressure, Brett keeps his cool in big games.

"After the first period, I was kind of starting to get a little nervous," Brett said. He knew that if he didn't score that night, his entrance into the exclusive 50-50 club would all be riding on the 50th game.

With less than two minutes left in the second period, Brett took a pass from teammate Jeff Brown. He paused briefly and then slammed the puck toward the opponent's goal. The shot flew past Detroit goalie Tim Cheveldae and landed in the Detroit net. Brett had scored goal number 49.

Even the Red Wing fans, watching their home team take a beating, had something to be excited about. When Brett landed another shot in the Detroit net early in the third period, the crowd came to its feet and cheered. Brett had scored his 50th goal and had taken his place in the hockey record books.

Brett was ecstatic. "I couldn't even play in the third period," he said. "I was in dreamland." Brett had more than one reason to be pleased. His team, the St. Louis Blues, was vying for the top spot in the NHL Norris Division. The Blues were having their best season in years. And the 50-50 milestone was just one of Brett Hull's many great achievements that season.

For years, when sports fans heard the name Hull, they thought of Bobby Hull, Brett's father. In the 1960s, Bobby Hull blazed his way into the NHL Hall of Fame as a star left winger for the Chicago Blackhawks.

But now things were changing. The name Hull was no longer just a reminder of a retired hockey legend. A new Hull was making his way to the top of the NHL.

Waiting in the Wings

Like many of hockey's top players, Brett Hull was born in Canada. In that nation, hockey is more popular than baseball or football. Many Canadian kids start to play hockey shortly after they learn to walk. And Brett was no exception.

It wasn't just Brett's nationality that got him into hockey at an early age. Unlike most young boys, Brett was the son of a famous hockey player. When Brett was born, his dad was playing for the Chicago Blackhawks. During the 1960s, Bobby Hull was considered by many to be the greatest goal scorer in the NHL.

What's more, Brett's mom, Joanne, was a figure-skating teacher and a former ice-show dancer. With his parents' encouragement, Brett was learning to skate by the age of three.

Brett was born on August 9, 1964, in Belleville, Ontario, where the Hull family had a cattle farm. The Hulls spent summers at the farm. But during the school year (and the hockey season), the family lived in Chicago. Brett and his older brothers, Bobby Jr. and Blake, liked to go to their father's games and practices. Afterwards, the elder Hull would give his sons pointers on skating and shooting.

"Watch and learn," Bobby would say.

Brett was lucky to have one of the NHL's best hockey players as his first teacher. Having a professional athlete for a father had its drawbacks, though. Bobby was constantly traveling, and he didn't have a lot of time for his family, which soon included Brett's younger brother, Bart, and sister, Michelle.

Bobby was rarely able to watch any of Brett's pee-wee hockey games. Brett recalls that when his father did attend a peewee game, the fans were far more interested in getting the great Bobby Hull's autograph than they were in watching the action on the ice.

In 1972, when Brett was eight, his family moved to Winnipeg, Manitoba, where Bobby Hull started to play with the Winnipeg Jets of the World Hockey Association. Brett continued to play hockey, baseball, and other organized sports. Opposing hockey players soon found out that Brett had inherited his father's powerful slap shot. New York Islander Richard Kromm remembers playing peewee hockey with Brett as a boy.

The three oldest Hull boys, Bobby Jr., Blake, and Brett (right), have fun on the ice at Chicago Stadium.

"Physically he was just a normal kid," Kromm says, "but he could really shoot the puck."

Despite his power, Brett wasn't a talented skater like his father. "He [Bobby] was so graceful," Brett remembers, "yet he didn't look like he was putting any effort into his skating."

Brett looked up to his father, whose illustrious career continued with the Jets. But the Hull family had its share of troubles.

Bobby Hull in
the 1960s

Bobby and Joanne Hull didn't have a happy marriage.
When Brett was 13 years old, his parents separated.
Brett and his siblings moved with their mother to
Vancouver, British Columbia, in western Canada.
Because Bobby Hull was famous in both Canada and
the United States, the divorce proceedings were well

publicized. It was painful for Brett to read articles about his parents' personal lives in the newspaper.

The marriage ended with bitter fighting, and Brett's parents severed all ties with one another. Bobby Hull stayed with the Jets for eight seasons, played briefly with the Hartford Whalers in Connecticut, and finally retired from hockey in 1980.

Brett, living with his mother in Vancouver, rarely heard from his dad. Brett missed his father, but he didn't blame him for keeping his distance from the rest of the family.

"Oh, yeah, he wasn't around, but it wasn't his fault," Brett comments. "Folks get divorced. You can't do anything about it. I was living with my mom, and I didn't go out of my way to see him either."

As a teenager, Brett played midget-league hockey. But no one thought Brett had a great future in the game. Despite his famous last name, professional scouts weren't interested in him. He hadn't distinguished himself on the ice, and he had a reputation for being lazy. "He'd always sit on the bench during the warm-ups," Brett's mother remembers. "He thought they were a waste of energy."

When Brett graduated from high school in 1982, he wasn't sure what to do next. He had not been a great student, so he didn't consider college. Brett still played hockey for fun, but he had few hopes for a professional hockey career.

Brett put his fierce slap shot to work for the Penticton Knights.

Brett also had a weight problem. With nearly 220 pounds (100 kilograms) on his 5-foot, 11-inch (180-centimeter) frame, Brett was slow and out of condition. He enjoyed heavy foods like steak, fried potatoes, and beer. Brett earned an unflattering nickname, "the Pickle," to match his bulging shape.

But a coach for an amateur team in British Columbia was willing to look past Brett's drawbacks. Coach Rick Kozuback of the Penticton Knights knew that Brett had a killer shot. Kozuback encouraged Brett to get in shape and offered him a spot on the team.

At Penticton, Brett's future started to look brighter. His skating improved, and he astounded everyone by scoring 105 goals in 56 games during the 1983-84 season. Although professional teams showed little interest in Brett, he began to hear from college hockey coaches. The University of Minnesota at Duluth offered Brett a scholarship to play for the school's hockey team, the Bulldogs. Brett accepted.

At Duluth, people began to compare Brett to his father. Few players measured up to Bobby Hull, who, with his fearsome slap shot, could send the puck into the opponent's goal at over 100 miles (161 kilometers) per hour.

It soon became clear that Brett had learned a few tricks from his dad. Brett began to set collegiate scoring records, and he earned nicknames like the Incredible Hull and the Great Brettzky—a flattering comparison to NHL star Wayne Gretzky, unquestionably the greatest player in all of hockey.

Brett worked out, ran, and improved his diet. He trimmed down to 200 pounds (91 kg), and his stamina and power increased. Brett would hit the puck so hard that he often broke several sticks per game.

At college, Brett often thought about his father. When Brett first joined the Bulldogs, he tacked up an old Bobby Hull trading card in his locker. Brett hoped that he and his dad would grow closer.

When Bobby Hull called to say he would be coming to watch the Bulldogs play in the 1985 season quarterfinals, Brett was thrilled. Bobby hadn't seen Brett play hockey in years. "You could see Brett light up when he heard his dad was coming," remembers Brett's roommate, Matt Christensen.

Bobby was not the only one pleased with Brett's performance at Duluth. The Calgary Flames had an eye on him. The Flames persuaded Brett to turn pro after his sophomore year. By the spring of 1986, Brett's professional hockey career was underway.

Golden Boy

Brett Hull describes himself as a laid-back guy. He seldom picks fights on the ice and stays clear of the brawls that often erupt during hockey games. "My personal philosophy has always been to expend more brain energy than body energy," he says. "I'm not real intense. I'm not intense at all."

Unfortunately for Brett, professional coaches aren't very laid back about their hockey players. When Brett reached Calgary in 1986, he was expected to work hard and practice hard. Yet Brett had a fondness for goofing off, sleeping late, and taking life easy. At the college level, he had made a name for himself as a goal scorer. He frequently stole the show with his powerful slap shot—but not much else.

Calgary Flame coach Terry Crisp wanted more from Brett. Crisp wanted Brett to work on his all-around game: defensive moves, checking, skating, and team strategy.

Brett (left) suited up in Calgary, but he didn't spend much time on the ice.

Coach Crisp wasn't pleased when Brett took it easy during the summer, showed up overweight at training camp, and didn't give his all at practice. Crisp had no patience with Brett. When Brett made a mistake, Crisp often lost his temper and pulled Brett out of the game. This hard-edged coaching style clashed dramatically with Brett's easy-going approach to hockey. Brett's performance suffered.

"It's really hard to play hockey knowing that when you make an error, you're going to get ripped," Brett complained. "You're trying to learn. You don't feel good when the coach is just ripping you."

Over the next two years, Brett played in only 57 games for the Flames. He spent most of 1986 and 1987 playing for Calgary's minor-league team and sat out during much of the 1987-88 season. Brett's 51-point total (27 goals and 24 assists) failed to impress the team's owners.

Brett was discouraged. When Calgary announced it would trade Brett and another player to the St. Louis Blues in March 1988, Brett wasn't very sorry to say goodbye. Brett felt that he had never been given a chance to prove himself with the Flames. He hadn't been very happy there.

"In Calgary, it was a veteran team and I didn't feel part of things," he said. "I knew they were on the verge [of winning a championship], but I didn't mind leaving."

Brett's new club, the St. Louis Blues, had its own problems. The Blues had a spotty record during the 1980s, and the team nearly moved out of town in 1983. St. Louis, Missouri, is well known for its baseball club, the Cardinals. When Brett came to town, few people in St. Louis were paying much attention to hockey.

But Brett was optimistic about signing on with the Blues. One reason for Brett's enthusiasm concerned his new coach, Brian Sutter. Sutter knew how to motivate his players. He worked with Brett, reviewing videos of games and suggesting ways in which Brett could improve.

Brett and Sutter worked well together. But Sutter wasn't easy on Brett. He still demanded discipline. He expected Brett to practice hard, keep his weight down, work on his defensive moves, and round out his game. This advice wasn't new to Brett. With Sutter's guidance, though, Brett was finally getting the message.

In his first full season with St. Louis, 1988-89, Brett made an impression with his big, powerful slap shot. He scored 41 goals and made 43 assists for a total of 84 points. He led the team in scoring and made the NHL All-Star team.

Sutter was pleased with Brett's progress, but he thought that Brett still didn't take his job seriously. Just blasting away at the opponent's net wasn't enough. Brett needed to be a team player. He needed to sharpen his skills. Sutter thought Brett had the potential to be a big star.

"I told him he could come back and score 40 goals again, or he could take the next step up and score 65," Sutter explained. "It was up to him and how hard he wanted to work."

"It was a turning point for me," Brett said. "My attitude up to that point was, 'Hey, I'm scoring, so they aren't going to get rid of me.'"

Coach Brian Sutter inspires Brett to play his best at all times.

With Sutter's direction, Brett stepped up his off-season training routine. He slimmed down to 195 pounds (88.5 kg) from a plump 205 (93 kg). He ran and lifted weights, and his endurance improved. Most importantly, Brett broadened his hockey skills. He worked on his wrist shots and became a more versatile offensive player.

The hard work paid off. During the next season, 1989-90, Brett had a league-leading 72 goals. This total was a record for right wingers. It was also big news on the hockey scene.

Wayne Gretzky held the overall record for goals in a season. He had tallied a sky-high 92 goals during his fourth season with the Edmonton Oilers. Brett's 72 goals fell far short of Gretzky's mark. But only five other NHL players had ever scored 70 or more goals in a season. Only Gretzky and Pittsburgh's Mario Lemieux had surpassed 80 goals per season. Now it looked as though Brett Hull might be closing in on these superstars.

But Brett's success wasn't just a one-man show. St. Louis was beginning to win more hockey games. Brett, teaming up with center Adam Oates, led the Blues to a 37-34-9 season. The win column wasn't enormous, but it showed an improvement over previous seasons. People in St. Louis were getting excited about hockey. Attendance at home games began to increase.

Brett, shadowed by a New York Ranger, looks for the puck.

Many people were starting to see gold in Brett Hull's future, and Brett renegotiated his contract with the Blues in June 1990. He would get upwards of $7 million over the next four seasons.

The Calgary Flames were soon to regret their decision to trade Brett a few years before. No one was calling Brett Hull lazy anymore. Now people were calling him the Golden Boy, and Brett set out to prove he was worthy of the title.

With Brett's 50th goal of the 1989-1990 season, Bobby and Brett
Hull became the first father and son to score 50 NHL goals.

26

The Incredible Hulls

Brett Hull bounds from center ice toward the opponent's net. Few would call Brett a graceful skater as he muscles his way across the ice with big, choppy strides. And though Brett is a capable stick handler, he rarely carries the puck for long before sending it on its way.

Brett is a difficult skater to keep up with, though. He's constantly dodging in and out of the action, giving defensemen the slip. And *that's* what makes Brett Hull such a good hockey player. He gets open. And when someone flips him the puck—bang! In an instant, Brett unleashes all the power of his killer slap shot.

"Hull is known for getting the puck in the slot and getting rid of it before you can blink," explains Adam Oates. "He's the most lethal weapon in the league."

"Brett Hull has the quickest release I've ever seen in hockey," adds Edmonton Oiler coach John Muckler. "The puck hits his stick and it's gone."

Professional hockey can be a brutal game. Most hockey players do not hesitate to plow into an opponent in order to wrestle the puck from his stick or knock him out of the play. Brett plays hard too, but he doesn't battle his way through a hockey game. He doesn't collect a lot of penalties for fighting.

Brett prefers to lurk outside the action, waiting for his chance to get open and get the puck. "He seems to be out of the play, and then the puck comes to him," marvels Calgary's Doug Gilmore. "The puck seems to find him no matter what."

Bobby Hull: The
Golden Jet

As longtime hockey fans watch Brett hustle across the ice, his blond hair sticking out from beneath his helmet, they probably remember another big, blond hockey player who made his mark as a scoring star. That powerhouse, of course, was Brett's dad, Bobby.

The elder Hull scored 913 goals in 23 seasons as a left winger for the Chicago Blackhawks, the Winnipeg Jets, and the Hartford Whalers. With the Blackhawks, Bobby Hull had five 50-goal seasons.

Bobby Hull is probably best known for the force of his slap shot. Bobby did not invent the shot, but he was one of the first players to show what a powerful weapon it could be.

To make a slap shot, a hockey player winds up and strikes the puck sharply, usually sending it flying through the air at a wicked speed. The slap shot is less accurate than the traditional wrist shot, but much harder to stop. When a slap shot flies toward the net, the goalie has only a split second to react.

At over 100 miles (161 km) per hour, Bobby Hull's slap shot was feared by goaltenders throughout the league. "When Hull shoots, I must not blink," NHL Hall of Famer Jacques Plante once said.

Bobby's shot wasn't the only thing that was fast. He could skate down the ice at 29 miles (47 km) per hour. Shortly after Bobby Hull hit the NHL, he earned a nickname, "the Golden Jet," to suit his blazing speed and bright blond hair.

Adam Oates springs into action. Brett (right) takes a quick rest.

Bobby disagrees. He thinks Brett has become the biggest name in all of hockey. "I used to be known as Bobby Hull, the Golden Jet," he says. "Now I'm Brett Hull's father."

Brett isn't the only one who has inherited athletic skill from Bobby. Brett's brother Blake is a top-ranked amateur golfer. Younger brother Bart played college football in the United States and professional football in Canada. Still, to most people, the name Hull will always mean hockey.

The Blue Streak

When the 1990-91 season began, St. Louis fans had big hopes for their team. Brett and the Blues were not about to let the fans down. The team quickly pushed its way to the top of the NHL standings.

Brett was excited. "We've got a young team that's on the upswing," he said. "Most of us came about the same time and we've built the team into a contender." For a club that had given lackluster performances in recent seasons, the turnaround was a dream come true.

And the head of the dream team was Brett Hull. Brett's enthusiasm on and off the ice and his ability to score big goals made him popular with his team-mates as well as the fans.

Brett was becoming a leader. And his tendency to keep clear of fights on the ice had made Brett a natural to win the Lady Byng Memorial Trophy as the league's "most gentlemanly player" the year before.

said. "To be on the list with those guys is quite a feeling."

Even so, Brett feels uncomfortable being compared to Gretzky, the hockey phenom who, playing for the Edmonton Oilers and the Los Angeles Kings, broke just about every hockey record. "I'm not even in his league," Brett says. "I'm just starting to be a good player."

While Brett was perfecting his act, Blues center Adam Oates was also piling up the points. Although Brett would end the season with the most goals, Adam would have many more assists. The Oates-to-Hull maneuver was responsible for a great many Blues goals.

Many people think that Brett Hull would never have racked up such big numbers without Adam Oates. Rather than shoot the puck himself, Adam often sets up a scoring play by passing the puck to Brett. "I wouldn't be the player I am without him," Brett admits.

Brett closed out the regular season with a staggering 86 goals—the third highest goal total of all time. This number, coupled with 45 assists, put Brett second only to Wayne Gretzky for total points that season.

Though he was pleased with his personal records, Brett was even more excited about the overall performance of his team. As the 1990-91 season was coming to a close, reporters asked Brett if he thought he could beat Gretzky's 92-goal record. Brett replied that he had other things on his mind.

In this Blues team photo, Brett is in the first row, second from the right.

"I haven't given it any thought," he said. "It would be pretty stupid not to want to get it, but we have 12 games left, and we're in a battle for first place."

That battle ended with the Chicago Blackhawks taking first in the division. But St. Louis fans were not disappointed with their team's second-place finish—just one point behind the Blackhawks. The team's 47-22-11 record was the best in club history. The fans waited eagerly for the post-season play-offs.

Adam Oates was Brett's scoring partner until he was traded to the
Boston Bruins in 1992.

Many people thought St. Louis had a good shot at the Stanley Cup.

In the first round of the play-offs, spirits stayed high. The Blues came from behind and knocked out the Detroit Red Wings in the Norris Division semifinals. The team went with confidence into a best-of-seven series against the Minnesota North Stars.

The North Stars were a shaky team with a poor record in the regular season. Most people were shocked that the Stars had made it into the second round of the play-offs by defeating Chicago. The Blues hoped to drop the North Stars in their tracks.

The contest began with a Minnesota victory, but the Blues quickly jumped back and tied the series 1-1. Then the North Stars won the next two games, and the St. Louis team started to get nervous.

The Blues had bounced back from a 3-1 deficit against Detroit in the semifinals, and now they needed to do it again. They needed three victories in a row. Brett tried to remain positive. "If we want to win, we'll win," he said. "We'll go out and do it, because we have a lot of class people."

St. Louis pulled off a 4-2 victory in the fifth game and kept the club's hopes alive. They held on in the sixth game, scoring twice with just under three minutes left to play. But the effort didn't pay off. The upstart North Stars bested St. Louis 3-2 and ended the series.

Minnesota had found the right approach to quieting the Blues: shut down Brett Hull. The North Stars assigned two men to check Brett and keep him off balance. He was held to just three goals in six games — far below his normal average.

The defeat left Brett and his teammates shaking their heads. The Blues had 20 more victories than Minnesota in the regular season. "It's hard not to be depressed," Brett said after the loss. "You work so hard and play so many games and sacrifice so much during the year [only] to lose this way."

Although the championship had escaped him, Brett's season accomplishments did not go unrecognized. He was named NHL player of the year by the *Sporting News*, and he won the Hart Trophy as the league's Most Valuable Player. With this award, Brett and Bobby Hull hooked up once more. They became the first father-son Hart Trophy winners. (Bobby had been named MVP in 1965 and 1966.)

Brett was honored to be chosen as the league's Most Valuable Player. And he was even prouder to join his dad on the MVP list.

"Everyone, when they grow up, tries to follow in their dad's footsteps," Brett said. "Whether they're hockey players, lawyers, doctors, or whatever.... He [Bobby] was the greatest left wing in the game. Maybe this [the Hart Trophy] is one of those things that brings me closer to the things he's done."

Despite his personal achievements, Brett was most interested in a victory for the team. Blues chairman Mike Shanahan summed it up well: "We've had a great season, and we have a lot to be proud of, but we wanted to give the fans a Stanley Cup."

But the championship continued to elude Brett and the St. Louis Blues. In the 1991-92 season, the team finished third in the Norris Division with a 36-33-11 record. They made it as far as the play-off semifinals that year, only to lose to the Chicago Blackhawks. Painful back spasms caused Brett to miss seven games that season and hampered his ability to help his team to victory. Still, Brett led the league with 70 goals for the year and reached a career record with a goals-per-game average of .807.

After a 37-36-11 season in 1992-93, the Blues battled their way through the division finals only to meet defeat against the Toronto Maple Leafs in the Stanley Cup play-offs.

Although the Blues finished with a respectable 40-33-11 record in the 1993-94 season, they were ousted in the first round of the Stanley Cup play-offs by the Dallas Stars. Brett, however, had an impressive season, becoming the Blues all-time goal scoring leader and scoring more than 50 goals for the fifth year in a row.

Even though the league championship continues to elude the Blues, hockey's top gun shows no sign of slowing down.

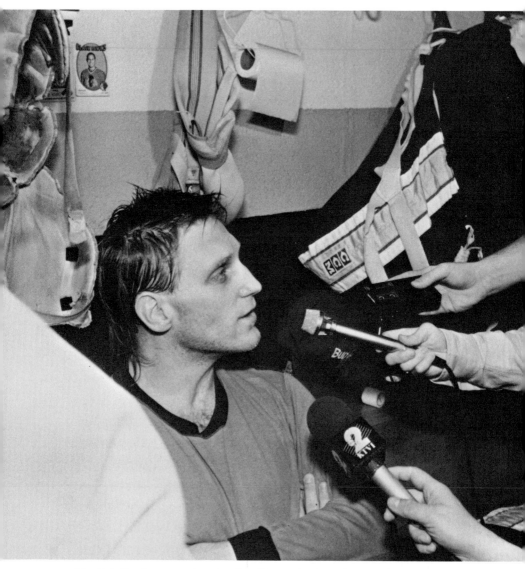

Brett talks to reporters in the Blues locker room. Bobby Hull's old hockey card is tacked up behind him.

Fanfare

At a shopping center in suburban St. Louis, people of all ages wait in line on a cold February afternoon. Hockey fans don't mind the long wait for a face-to-face meeting with Brett Hull.

Brett can often be found at the St. Louis Arena signing autographs—long after his teammates have already gone home after a game. More than 1,000 letters pour into the Blues publicity office each week with requests for a photo, a signature, or a word from Brett Hull. The letters come from all over the world.

At first Brett was perplexed about being a hero. "It's weird. I look at all the famous people, and kids want to be me?...I'm just a normal guy," Brett argues. But Brett is starting to realize that big sports stars aren't able to lead normal, quiet lives.

Most famous hockey players are from Canada. Even if they play in the United States, many of the NHL's biggest stars are Canadian citizens. Brett was born in Canada too. But since Brett's mother is an American, Brett has dual U.S.-Canadian citizenship.

When Brett said he would play for the United States in the 1991 Canada Cup tournament, hockey fans were excited. Usually, the best hockey players team up with Canada. The star-studded Canadian team won the last two tournaments, which were held in 1984 and 1987. The U.S. team, though, finished a distant fourth and fifth (out of six teams). Some Canadians were unhappy to see Brett join up with the American team. But in the United States, hockey fans couldn't have been happier.

Brett is bringing new American interest to hockey, which often takes a back seat to big-league baseball, football, and basketball. In St. Louis, thousands of people crowd into the Brentwood Ice Rink just to watch Brett and the Blues practice! Big companies, including Coca-Cola, have hired Brett to endorse their products.

It's no wonder that Brett Hull is also popular off the ice. Brett is friendly and outgoing. He also has cobalt-blue eyes, dimples, and a charming smile. Some female fans are disappointed to learn that Brett has a girlfriend, Allison Curran, whom he met when he was in college in Duluth.

Brett in his college days

Brett and Allison live in suburban St. Louis. During the off-season, they spend time at their lake home in northern Minnesota. Brett still loves to relax. He works hard on the ice, but when he leaves the rink he wants nothing more than to unplug the phone, lounge in front of his big-screen TV, listen to one of his 300 rock music CDs, or get out on the golf course.

When he's not playing hockey or practicing his golf swing, Brett can sometimes be seen driving around town in one of his three cars. With the stereo cranked up in his Chevrolet Blazer, red Corvette, or Nissan Infiniti Q45, Brett is sure to be noticed. But he enjoys being a star. He happily jokes with reporters and has recently appeared on several talk shows, including "Late Night with David Letterman."

What's next for hockey's top gun? Most of all, he wants to be a champion. "I'm trying to hone my skills," Brett says, "and if I do, maybe I can win a Stanley Cup. . . . I'll give it my best."

Brett also has goals outside of hockey. In fact, he'd even like to try acting. "I think it would be the coolest thing to be a movie star," he says. "I could do a Western. That would be awesome."

For now, Brett is far more likely to be starring on the sports channel than on a movie screen. "There's nothing I enjoy more than scoring goals," he says.

"When I . . . see those 18,000 people in their seats and I know they're cheering for me, it gives me goose pimples. . . . You want to go back out there and score another goal, just to have that feeling again."

BRETT HULL
Hockey statistics

University of Minnesota-Duluth

YEAR	GAMES	GOALS	ASSISTS	POINTS	PENALTY MINUTES
1984-85	48	32	28	60	24
1985-86	42	52	32	84	46

Calgary Flames

YEAR	GAMES	GOALS	ASSISTS	POINTS	PENALTY MINUTES
1986-87	5	1	0	1	0
1987-88	52	26	24	50	12

St. Louis Blues

Regular season

YEAR	GAMES	GOALS	ASSISTS	POINTS	PENALTY MINUTES
1988-89	78	41	43	84	33
1989-90	80	72	41	113	24
1990-91	78	86	45	131	22
1991-92	73	70	39	109	48
1992-93	80	54	47	101	41
1993-94	81	57	40	97	38

Play-offs

YEAR	GAMES	GOALS	ASSISTS	POINTS	PENALTY MINUTES
1988-89	10	5	5	10	6
1989-90	12	13	8	21	17
1990-91	13	11	8	19	4
1991-92	6	4	4	8	4
1992-93	11	8	5	13	2
1993-94	4	2	1	3	0

ACKNOWLEDGMENTS

Photographs reproduced with permission of Mark Buckner, pp. 1, 2, 6, 8, 23, 25, 26, 31, 32, 37, 38, 42, 46; University of Minnesota-Duluth, p. 10; Chicago Blackhawks, pp. 13, 14, 28; *Vancouver Sun*, pp. 16 (Ken Oakes), 20 (Ralph Bower); Pittsburgh Penguins, p. 34; Doug Maclellan, p. 35; *Vancouver Province*, p. 45 (David Clark). Cover photographs by Mark Buckner.